YOU KNOW YOU ARE

A MOTHER...

by Richard McChesney

illustrated by Scooter McKenzie

You Know You Are A Mother... will have mothers everywhere nodding in agreement as they realize just how talented and forgiving they have become.

This is the eighth book in the "You Know You Are" book series, and is dedicated to mothers everywhere. On behalf of your children, thanks for everything you do.

Other books in the "You Know You Are" series are:

- You Know You Are A Runner...
- You Know You Are A Nurse...
- You Know You Are An Engineer...
- You Know You Are A Dog Lover...
- You Know You Are A Golfer...
- You Know You Are Getting Older...
- You Know You Are A Teacher...

Visit www.YouKnowYouAreBooks.com to join our mailing list and be notified when future titles are released, or find us at www.facebook.com/YouKnowYouAreBooks, or follow us on twitter (@YouKnowYouAreBK)

You Know You Are A Mother...

First edition published 2014 by Strictly Business Limited

Happy reading!

STRICTLY
BUSINESS

ISBN 978-1-909943-07-0

YOU KNOW YOU ARE A MOTHER
WHEN THE MOST EXCITING SOCIAL EVENTS
YOU ATTEND ARE THE PARENT TEACHER
MEETINGS AT THE SCHOOL!...

YOU KNOW YOU ARE A MOTHER
WHEN YOU CAN TURN OUT A COSTUME FOR
TOMORROW'S SCHOOL DRESS-UP DAY WHEN
YOU ONLY FOUND OUT ABOUT IT AT BEDTIME...

YOU KNOW YOU ARE A MOTHER
WHEN YOUR 'ME TIME' CONSISTS OF DADDY
WATCHING THE BABY FOR 30 MINUTES WHILE
YOU CLEAN UP THE KITCHEN...

YOU KNOW YOU ARE A MOTHER
WHEN BABY WIPES ARE MORE
VALUABLE THAN MONEY...

YOU KNOW YOU ARE A MOTHER
WHEN THERE IS AN EMAIL SITTING IN YOUR
INBOX TITLED 'HEAD LICE'...

YOU KNOW YOU ARE A MOTHER
WHEN PEANUT BUTTER AND JELLY FEATURE
IN AT LEAST ONE MEAL A DAY...

YOU KNOW YOU ARE A MOTHER
WHEN YOU ARE AN EXPERT AT CUTTING
GUM OUT OF HAIR...

YOU KNOW YOU ARE A MOTHER
WHEN THE CLOSEST YOU GET TO GOURMET
COOKING IS MAKING RICE KRISPIE TREATS...

YOU KNOW YOU ARE A MOTHER
WHEN YOU PUT ON MAKEUP AND THE KIDS
GET EXCITED THAT YOU'RE <u>ALL</u> GOING OUT...

YOU KNOW YOU ARE A MOTHER
WHEN THE LAST THING YOU DO
ON A VACATION IS RELAX...

YOU KNOW YOU ARE A MOTHER
WHEN YOU CAN TAKE A SHOWER AND DO
HAIR & MAKEUP IN LESS THAN 10 MINUTES...

YOU KNOW YOU ARE A MOTHER
WHEN YOU CAN SLEEP RIGHT THROUGH A
STORM BUT WAKE UP TO THE SLIGHTEST
NOISE FROM ONE OF YOUR KIDS...

YOU KNOW YOU ARE A MOTHER
WHEN YOU CAN DO 6 DIFFERENT THINGS
AT THE SAME TIME...

YOU KNOW YOU ARE A MOTHER
WHEN YOUR CHILDREN THINK OF YOU AS
THEIR PERSONAL TAXI DRIVER...

YOU KNOW YOU ARE A MOTHER
WHEN YOU FIND YOURSELF CUTTING YOUR PARTNER'S SANDWICHES INTO CUTE SHAPES...

YOU KNOW YOU ARE A MOTHER
WHEN YOU DON'T THINK TWICE ABOUT EATING
THE FOOD YOUR CHILD DROPPED...

YOU KNOW YOU ARE A MOTHER
WHEN YOU COUNT THE SPRINKLES
ON EACH KID'S CUPCAKE TO MAKE
SURE THEY'RE EQUAL...

YOU KNOW YOU ARE A MOTHER
WHEN YOU COOK AS MUCH WITH THE PLAY
KITCHEN AS THE REAL ONE...

YOU KNOW YOU ARE A MOTHER
WHEN YOU HAVE SNIFFED YOUR CHILD'S
BUTT IN PUBLIC...

YOU KNOW YOU ARE A MOTHER
WHEN YOU HAVE CRAWLED UNDER A CRIB AT
2 A.M. SEARCHING FOR A PACIFIER LIKE
YOUR LIFE DEPENDED ON IT...

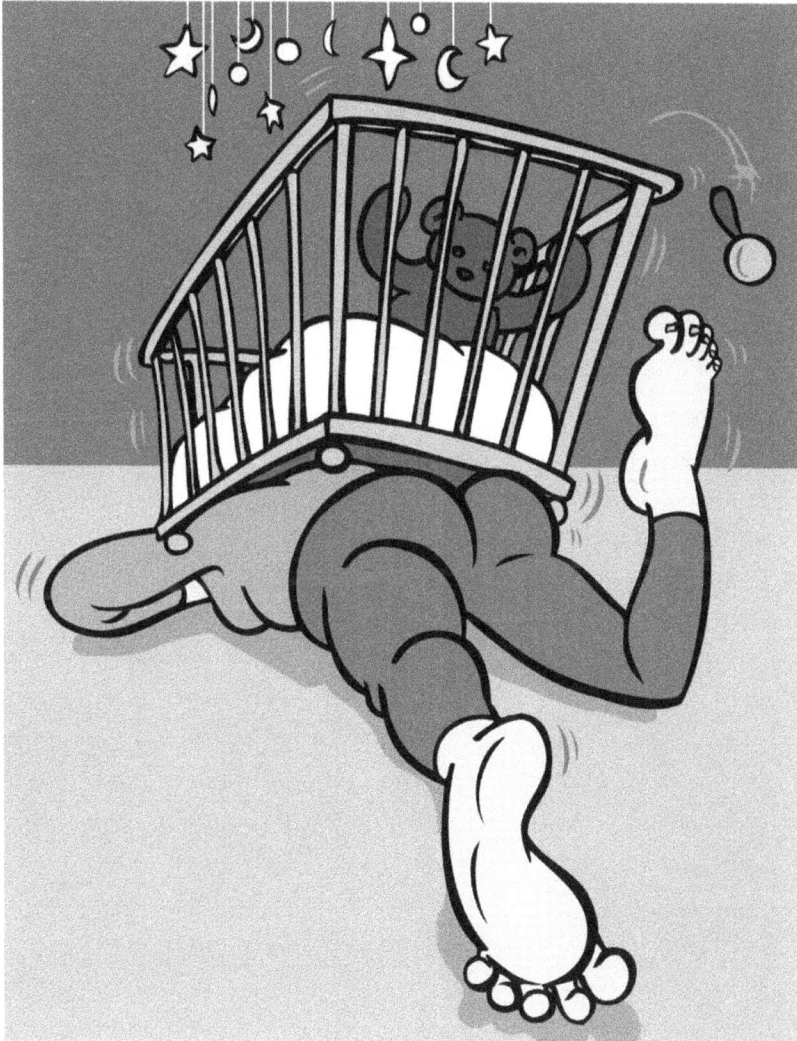

YOU KNOW YOU ARE A MOTHER
WHEN YOUR IDEA OF A GOOD DAY IS MAKING
IT THROUGH WITHOUT A CHILD LEAKING
BODILY FLUIDS ON YOU...

YOU KNOW YOU ARE A MOTHER
WHEN YOU HEAR YOUR MOTHER'S VOICE
COMING OUT OF YOUR MOUTH WHEN YOU
SAY, "NOT IN YOUR GOOD CLOTHES!"...

YOU KNOW YOU ARE A MOTHER
WHEN YOU HAVE TRIED AT LEAST ONCE TO
PUT YOUR HUSBAND IN TIME OUT...

YOU KNOW YOU ARE A MOTHER
WHEN YOU HAVE STARTED REFERRING
TO YOUR HUSBAND AS "DADDY" RATHER
THAN BY HIS NAME...

YOU KNOW YOU ARE A MOTHER
WHEN YOU STICK A BOTTLE IN THE MOUTH
OF ANYONE THAT IS UPSET...

YOU KNOW YOU ARE A MOTHER
WHEN YOU JUDGE THE QUALITY OF A
RESTAURANT BY HOW THEY ACT WHEN YOUR
KID MAKES A MESS ON THE FLOOR...

YOU KNOW YOU ARE A MOTHER
WHEN YOU HIRE A SITTER BECAUSE YOU
HAVEN'T BEEN OUT WITH YOUR HUSBAND IN
AGES, THEN SPEND HALF THE NIGHT
CHECKING ON THE KIDS...

YOU KNOW YOU ARE A MOTHER
WHEN YOU HIDE IN THE BATHROOM
TO BE ALONE...

YOU KNOW YOU ARE A MOTHER
WHEN YOU WAKE UP WITH THE
WHOLE FAMILY NEXT TO YOU...

YOU KNOW YOU ARE A MOTHER
WHEN YOU USE YOUR OWN SALIVA TO
CLEAN YOUR CHILD'S FACE...

YOU KNOW YOU ARE A MOTHER
WHEN YOU THINK SINGING 'RUDOLPH THE RED-NOSED REINDEER' AT BEDTIME EVERY NIGHT YEAR-ROUND IS COMPLETELY RATIONAL...

YOU KNOW YOU ARE A MOTHER
WHEN YOU TAKE A NAP WHEN
YOUR BABY DOES...

YOU KNOW YOU ARE A MOTHER
WHEN YOU'RE SO DESPERATE FOR ADULT
CONVERSATION THAT YOU SPILL YOUR GUTS
TO THE TELEMARKETER THAT CALLS...

YOU KNOW YOU ARE A MOTHER
WHEN YOUR KISSES HAVE MAGICAL,
HEALING PROPERTIES...

YOU KNOW YOU ARE A MOTHER

WHEN YOUR KIDS MAKE JOKES ABOUT BODILY
FUNCTIONS, AND YOU THINK IT'S FUNNY...

YOU KNOW YOU ARE A MOTHER
WHEN YOUR KID THROWS-UP
AND YOU CATCH IT...

YOU KNOW YOU ARE A MOTHER
WHEN A TRIP TO THE GROCERY STORE ALONE
IS YOUR IDEA OF A SPONTANEOUS GETAWAY...

So... are you a
Mother?

You have just read the eighth book in the "You Know You Are" series.

Other "You Know You Are" books are:

- You Know You Are A Runner...
- You Know You Are A Nurse...
- You Know You Are An Engineer...
- You Know You Are A Dog Lover...
- You Know You Are A Golfer...
- You Know You Are Getting Older...
- You Know You Are A Teacher...

If you enjoyed this book why not join our mailing list to be notified when future titles are released – visit www.YouKnowYouAreBooks.com, or find us on facebook (www.facebook.com/YouKnowYouAreBooks), or follow us on twitter (@YouKnowYouAreBK)

Other 'You Know You Are' books include:

Visit www.YouKnowYouAreBooks.com for further details.

www.ingramcontent.com/pod-product-compliance
Lightning Source LLC
Chambersburg PA
CBHW071626040426
42452CB00009B/1508